LET'S GET ZAPPING...

SO WHAT SHOULD YOU BE ZAPPING IN THE ANNUAL?

Wherever you see the **interactive icon** you'll be able to unlock a fun experience to enjoy on your device. There are 15 scattered throughout the book to discover.

See if you can find them all.

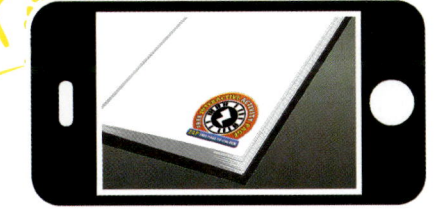

READY.
Open Zappar on your device and find the Zapcode in the menu.

AIM.
Tap the Zapcode icon in the menu and scan the code on the page to download the content to your device.

ZAP.
Then point your device at the page and watch it come to life.

A FEW HELPFUL TIPS...

To get the best possible experience here are a few hints and tips:

- Connect to wifi if you can and the experiences will download even quicker than on 3G.
- Try and keep the pages as flat as you can for the best effect. Rest the book on a table or on the floor.
- Try and keep the full page in view from your phone after scanning the code. Don't get too close or far away if you can help it.
- Try and keep the pages clean and free from tears, pen and other marks as this may affect the experience.
- It's best to view the pages in good lighting conditions if you can.

If you're still having problems then do contact us at **support@zappar.com** and we'll do our best to help you.

ZeptoLab, Cut the Rope, Cut the Rope: Experiments, Om Nom, Nommies and Feed with Candy are the trademarks or registered trademarks of ZeptoLab UK Limited. © 2013. All rights reserved.

Contents

- Welcome 06
- Profile: Om Nom 08
  - Profile: Evan 10
  - Profile: Haley 11
  - Profile: Spider 12
  - Profile: Snail 13
  - Profile: Professor 14
  - Join the Club! 16
- Om Nom grid drawing 18
  - A–Z of Cut the Rope 20
- Maze Muddle 22
- COMIC: Strange Delivery Part One ... 24
  - Wordsearch 32
- Box Bungle 33
  - Om Nom's Big Quiz 34
  - Spot the Difference 36
- Sliding Sweets 37
  - Om Nom's 'Feed Me' Flip Book ... 38
- Colour By Numbers 40
- Cut the Rope Posters 42
  - Time Travel Board Game 44
- Time Tangle 46
- How to Draw Om Nom 47
- Shadow Match 48
  - Anagrams 50
- Sweet Thief! 51
- COMIC: Strange Delivery Part Two ... 52
  - Everybody Loves Om Nom! 60
  - Doughnut Drop 62
  - Cookie Cutter 64
  - Feed Me NOW! 66
  - What's in the Box? 67
  - Comical Candy 68
  - Sweet Sudoku 70
- Odd One Out 71
  - Creative Catchphrase 72
  - Extreme Close-up! 73
  - Brilliant Boxes 74
- Jelly Jigsaw 76
  - Answers 77

> Unlock bonus interactive features.

Pedigree

Published 2013. Pedigree Books Limited, Beech Hill House, Walnut Gardens, Exeter, Devon EX4 4DH.
www.pedigreebooks.com — books@pedigreegroup.co.uk
The Pedigree trademark, email and website addresses, are the sole and exclusive properties of Pedigree Group Limited, used under licence in this publication.

Welcome

Om Nom's first annual is packed with games, stories and fun things to make and do. But watch out — there are also ten tiny spiders trying to steal Om Nom's candy! The spiders are hiding among the activities. When you spot them, write the page numbers here.

Om Nom can't wait for you to start playing with him — and feeding him candy!

OM NOM

Sharp teeth for chomping candy

Big eyes for spotting candy

Four fast feet for running to safety

Om Nom is a friendly green monster who loves sweet things. He's very shy and loud noises scare him, but he's a loyal and funny friend.

No one knows where Om Nom came from. He just turned up one day in a box on Evan's doorstep. He can't talk, so his friends can't ask him questions. All they can do is care for him, feed him candy and have fun.

Om Nom's sweet tooth often gets him into trouble. He never means to be naughty, but somehow mess and mischief seem to follow him around!

Favourite food: Candy
Best friend: Evan
Arch enemy: Spider
Biggest fear: Evan's cat
Favourite colour: Green

IF YOU COULD ASK OM NOM ONE QUESTION, WHAT WOULD IT BE?

Evan

Evan is twelve years old. He lives in an ordinary town and he goes to an ordinary school, and so far his life has been pretty boring. But now Om Nom has turned up, things have suddenly got very exciting indeed!

Favourite activity: Watching TV
Best friend: Haley
Most embarrassed by: Everything his parents do.
Favourite food: Pizza
Favourite TV: The X Files

When Evan's not feeding Om Nom or getting him out of trouble, he's trying to figure out where the little green guy came from. He also has to find time to do his homework, tidy his room and hang out with his friend Haley. It's ages since he had the chance to slump in front of the TV!

Haley

Haley is pretty and cool, and she thinks Evan is a bit weird, but she likes him because he's different. She goes to school with Evan, and she shares his amazing secret.

Favourite activity: Swimming
Most embarrassed by: Evan's clumsy antics.
Favourite animals: Dogs
Favourite TV: Mysteries and adventures

Haley loves the adventures she and Evan have together, and they both really care about Om Nom.

11

Spider

Greedy Spider longs to eat all Om Nom's candy. But Om Nom's friends keep getting in his way! He's very quick and he can always sense when sweets are nearby. All those legs help him to grab as much candy as possible.

Favourite food: Candy
Best friend: Himself
Arch enemy: Om Nom
Biggest fear: Spider splatters
Favourite colour: Black

Snail

Snail lives underwater and spends most of his time asleep. When he wakes up, he likes watching the fish and helping his friend Om Nom. He's timid, but he'll do everything he can to keep Spider away from the candy. Sometimes he even hides it in the aquarium!

Favourite food: Leaves and plants
Best friends: The fish in the aquarium
Arch enemy: None
Biggest fear: Speed
Favourite colour: Orange

The Professor

White lab coat

Mad scientist hair

Bony fingers

The Professor lives next door to Evan, and he thinks Om Nom is amazing! He wants to understand everything about the little green monster. His weird and wonderful experiments are designed to find out why Om Nom loves candy so much.

The Professor finds it hard to think about anything except science. He often forgets to eat and he isn't interested in making friends. He just wants to find as many ways as possible to feed Om Nom with candy.

Favourite activity: Doing scientific experiments

Cares most about: His laboratory and scientific equipment

Most irritated by: Interruptions to his work

IF THE PROFESSOR WOULD DO AN EXPERIMENT FOR YOU, WHAT WOULD YOU LIKE HIM TO FIND OUT?

Join the Club!

Follow these simple steps to make your own Om Nom badge. Then invent an Om Nom fan club for you and your friends!

You will need
- Pencil
- White card
- Scissors
- An adult to help you
- Colouring pens
- Safety pin
- Sticky tape

1 Choose a badge template.

2 Use a pencil to copy the template onto a piece of white card.

3 Colour in the picture and the words. Make the badge as bright and interesting as you can!

4 Ask an adult to help you cut out the badge.

5 Use sticky tape to attach the safety pin to the back of the badge.

6 Wear your badge with pride!

DELIVER CANDY HERE

Feed with Candy

Cut above the rest

Feed me NOW!

Always ask an adult to help you when using scissors and safety pins.

Om Nom has arrived on your doorstep!

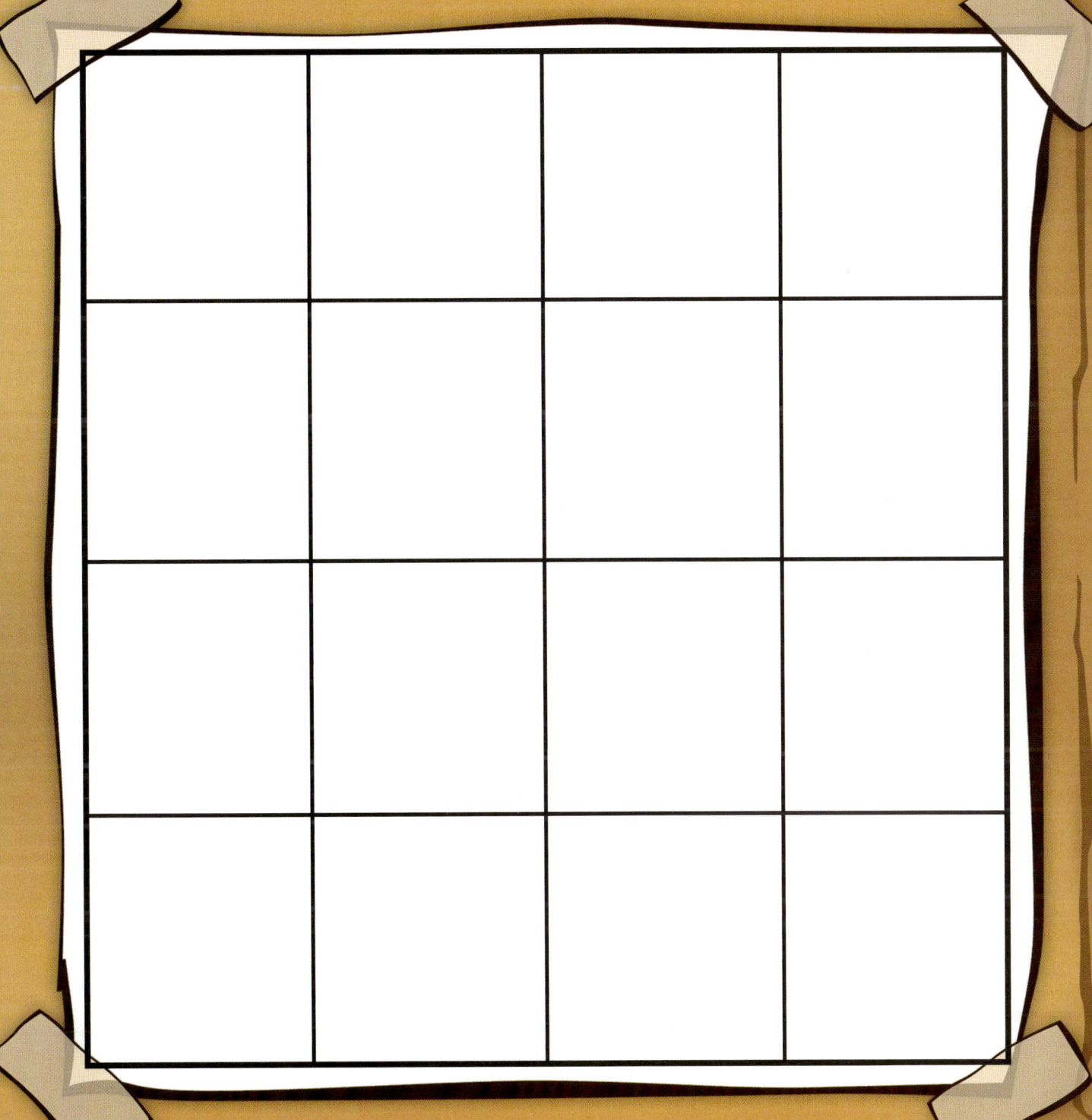

Copy this picture of your new friend one square at a time, and then colour it in.

Cut the Rope A to Z

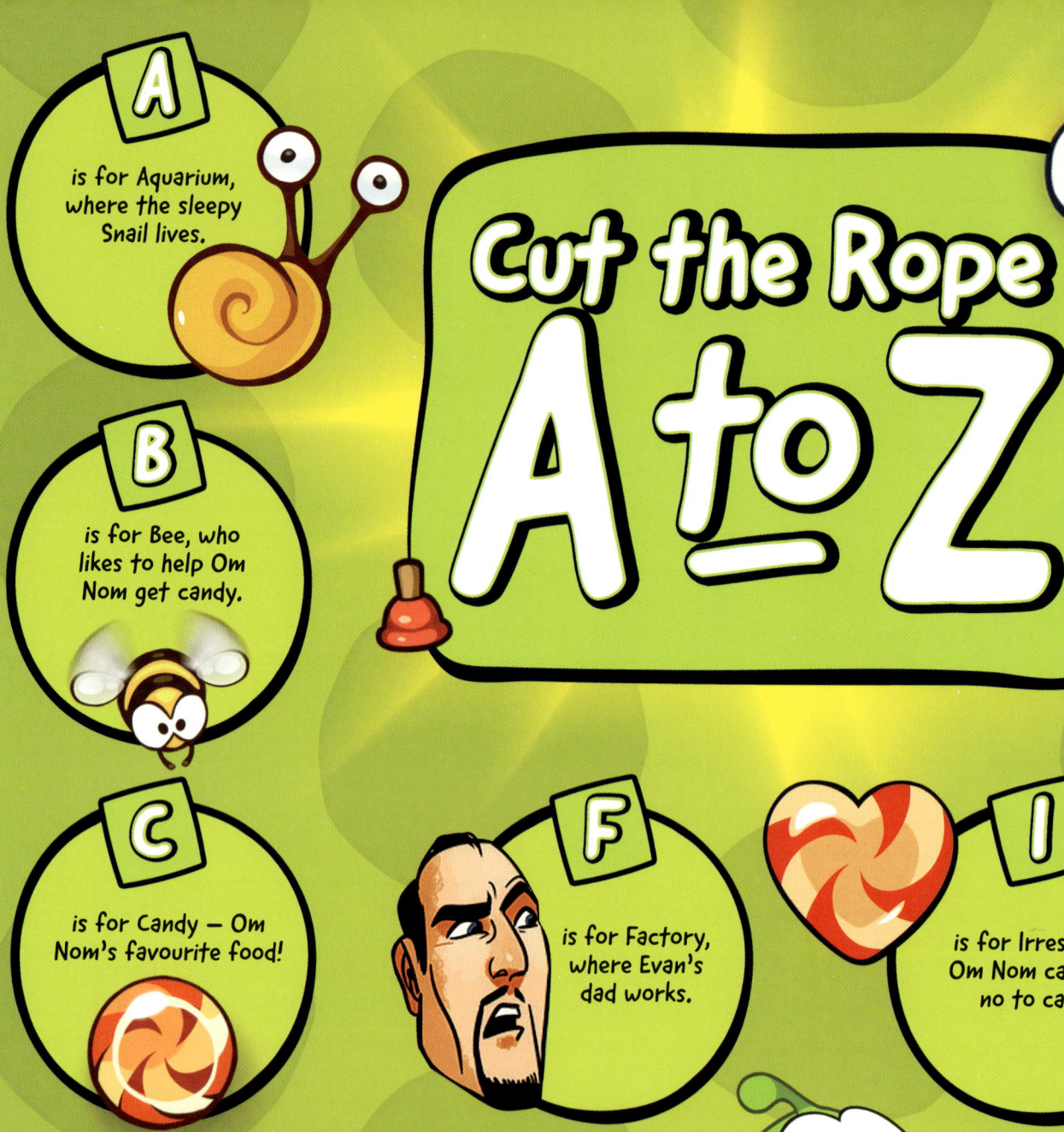

A is for Aquarium, where the sleepy Snail lives.

B is for Bee, who likes to help Om Nom get candy.

C is for Candy — Om Nom's favourite food!

D is for Dentist, which is Evan's mum's job.

E is for Evan. He's Om Nom's best friend and he makes sure the little monster gets enough candy.

F is for Factory, where Evan's dad works.

G is for Green, the best colour for a little monster!

H is for Haley. She helps Evan to care for Om Nom.

I is for Irresistible. Om Nom can't say no to candy!

J is for Jokes. Evan likes trying to make Om Nom laugh.

K is for Kind. You must be kind to your little green friend if you want to keep him happy.

L is for Label. The label on Om Nom's box tells you what he likes to eat!

Feed with Candy

Q is for Questions. The Professor has lots of questions about Om Nom.

V is for Valentine box, where Om Nom plays Cupid.

M is for Monster — and the Mystery of where he came from!

R is for Rope, which the Professor uses to deliver candy to Om Nom.

W is for What's inside the box?

N is for New Friends. Will you be Om Nom's friend?

S is for Spider, Om Nom's arch enemy.

X is for 'X marks the spot where the candy is hidden!'

O is for Om Nom of course!

T is for Top Hat. Om Nom likes to look smart!

Y is for Yum Yum. Om Nom likes eating!

P is for Professor. He wants to find out everything about the little monster.

U is for Unexpected Delivery. Om Nom turned up on Evan's doorstep in a box!

Z is for Zoo. People might put Om Nom in a zoo if they found him, so Evan, Haley and the Professor have to keep him secret!

Maze Muddle

Om Nom is hungry! But Spider and his friends are hungry too, and they want to stop Om Nom from reaching the candy. Can you help him to find his sweets without bumping into any spiders?

START

FINISH

Strange Delivery

Part 1

AHHHH!

UNLESS YOU ARE SELLING COOKIES I'M NOT...

HUH?
LOOKS LIKE MOM WENT ON ANOTHER HOME SHOPPING BINGE.
RUSTLE
RUSTLE
WHA...?
DID SOMEONE MAIL A CAT...?
AHH!

SPRING!
SPRING!
SPRING!
WHOAH... HEY...
OH...NOT THE KITCHEN. PLEASE NOT THE KITCHEN.

WELL...
Feed with Candy.
...MISSION ACCOMPLISHED.
WHAT AM I GONNA TELL MOM AND DAD?
OUR HERO HAS FACED CHALLENGES BEFORE, BUT NONE CAN MATCH THE SHEER VILLAINY OF...
...THE GREEN SQUISHY THING THAT ATE ALL THE GOOD FOOD IN THE HOUSE!

FREEZE! DON'T MOVE!
STOP RIGHT THERE!
MAN, DO NONE OF THE PHRASES FROM COP SHOWS WORK?
I GOT YO...
...OOOOOO... OW!
RIIIIP!
YOU... YOU TRIED TO HELP ME?
...
THANKS.
WAIT! WHERE ARE YOU GOING?

WHO ARE YOU AND WHAT ARE YOU DOING IN MY POOL?
YOU BETTER DRY OF-- ...YIKES!
"YIKES?" WHAT'S WRO--
GRRRRRRRRRR
GRRRR
YAH! WHAT THE MONKEY TAIL IS THAT?
DON'T WORRY ABOUT THAT, IT'S DRUMMOND'S THREE EVIL ROTTWIELERS. THEY GROWL LIKE THAT WHENEVER THEY'VE...
QUICK, GET SOME CANDY!
SMACK!

WHAT DO YOU MEAN IT'S GONE?!?
...THAT IS...UM...TO SAY...
ACTUALLY...UH... SIR, QUITE FRANKLY WE DON'T KNOW WHAT EXACTLY HAPPENED.
ALL WE DO KNOW IS THAT SOMETIME BETWEEN THE SUBJECT'S 2:10 AND 2:15 FEEDING, IT DISAPPEARED.
WELL THEN...
...FIND IT!
WE'VE COME TOO FAR FOR PROJECT: NUTRILICIOUS TO BE JEOPARDIZED NOW.
YES SIR.

HI HALEY!
HI EVAN!
I WAS HOPING THAT YOU MIGHT BE ABLE TO TALK FOR A FEW MINUTES?
SO, IT WASN'T A CAT. IT WASN'T A DOG. ARE YOU GOING TO TELL ME WHAT IT IS? OR DO I HAVE TO KEEP GUESSING?
WOW...
WHAT IS IT?
I DON'T KNOW. HE JUST SHOWED UP ON MY DOORSTEP EARLIER.
WELL, I'M GOING TO HELP YOU SOLVE THIS MYSTERY.
YOU'VE APPARENTLY HAD A BUSY FIRST WEEK ON THE JOB.
YOU ARE TOO NEW AND INCONSEQUENTIAL TO BIG VEGETABLE INC. TO COMPREHEND THE SIGNIFICANCE OF THE SUBJECT.
AS SUCH, I'M SURE YOU WERE INSTRUCTED TO STEAL FROM ME.
SO, I'LL MAKE THIS REAL EASY FOR YOU.
I DON'T CARE THAT YOU TOOK THE SUBJECT. I JUST WANT TO KNOW WHO TOLD YOU TO AND WHERE YOU TOOK IT.
IF YOU TELL ME I PROMISE YOU, YOU CAN WALK OUT THE DOOR UNHARMED. IF YOU DON'T TELL ME, THEN I CAN'T MAKE THAT PROMISE.
OKAY MAN...IT'S NO BIGGIE TO ME...I'LL TELL YOU...
FREE INTERACTIVE STORY PAGE
ZAP THIS PAGE TO UNLOCK

WORDSEARCH

Ten different types of delicious food are hidden in this grid. Are you hungry enough to find them all?

W	A	G	T	M	A	I	T	E	O	A	L	C	O	E	S	E	T	A	I
S	O	S	B	E	N	A	C	Y	D	N	A	C	S	M	N	Y	E	P	E
I	U	S	H	J	S	D	N	U	E	S	N	A	D	L	G	C	U	M	Y
E	Y	Y	U	E	I	E	I	V	I	N	Y	T	I	N	C	S	L	D	O
T	I	S	E	N	R	T	R	Y	H	M	F	Y	L	L	E	J	S	J	V
F	M	C	S	R	N	B	S	R	O	T	U	A	I	W	L	L	K	M	T
S	E	H	J	S	N	H	E	K	N	S	I	S	M	D	A	Y	I	H	O
O	N	O	A	E	D	B	U	T	O	N	N	A	C	H	A	N	L	P	O
R	I	C	S	D	O	U	G	H	N	U	T	G	A	R	T	E	I	F	K
H	R	O	S	F	W	N	C	S	T	D	S	W	E	S	I	S	U	J	K
G	N	L	W	Z	C	B	T	V	U	V	H	E	S	R	U	U	G	H	J
R	W	A	H	J	S	S	G	I	O	O	G	S	C	H	B	S	V	H	
I	U	T	P	O	N	U	E	A	I	T	L	M	S	R	S	H	U	H	E
B	I	E	D	O	E	V	K	T	A	E	V	K	A	T	A	A	H	W	U
Z	A	E	B	C	D	M	A	C	T	L	P	T	I	E	E	I	E	Y	L
U	P	N	P	E	J	O	C	V	E	K	K	B	F	G	R	A	T	R	A
W	O	L	T	E	M	L	P	H	T	O	F	F	E	E	J	C	I	N	T
B	H	L	R	V	D	B	U	A	W	P	Q	Y	D	O	C	X	E	H	J
R	C	L	Q	W	F	G	C	F	X	G	X	F	U	G	K	S	O	C	T
C	V	J	W	O	N	B	R	Y	J	P	S	K	M	E	U	I	G	R	I

- Bonbons
- Chocolate
- Doughnut
- Jelly
- Sherbet
- Candy cane
- Cupcake
- Ice cream
- Mints
- Toffee

32

Box Bungle

Om Nom has different outfits to match his different boxes. Can you guess which outfit belongs with which box? Draw lines to match the pairs, and then write the correct name under each box.

Om Nom's Big Quiz

How much do you know about Om Nom and his favourite food? You need to be an expert if you are going to look after him well. Answer these questions to find out how sweet-smart you really are!

1 Who lives next door to Evan?

2 The main ingredients of cake are eggs, flour, butter and ....?

3 What is Evan's mum's job?

4 Marzipan is made of sugar and ....

5 Who works in a sweet factory?

6 What is this sweet called?

7 Where does Snail live?

8 Who always tries to steal Om Nom's sweets?

9 What does Om Nom live inside?

10 At what time of year might a bunny give you chocolate eggs?

NOW CHECK YOUR ANSWERS AND WRITE DOWN YOUR SCORE.

My score is   /10

1–5 Sour! You need to pay a little more attention to Om Nom's needs. Read the annual again and then re-take the quiz. Good luck!

6–8 Savoury! You've done well, but there is room for improvement. Keep feeding Om Nom and observing his likes and dislikes. Soon you'll know as much about him as Evan does!

9–10 Sweet! Very few people are as clever as you. Perhaps you should think about joining the Professor in his lab. You've definitely got geek potential!

35

Spot the Difference

Evan has been taking some photos of the Professor's experiments. But there's something weird about this camera! These photos look the same, but there are ten differences between them. Can you spot them all?

A

B

36

SLIDING SWEETS

Om Nom can't eat his candy until you put this picture back together in the right way. Stop his tummy from rumbling by completing the puzzle in record time. When you work out where each piece belongs, write the numbers in the grid.

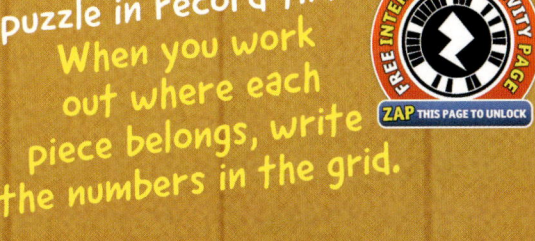

FREE INTERACTIVE ACTIVITY PAGE — ZAP THIS PAGE TO UNLOCK

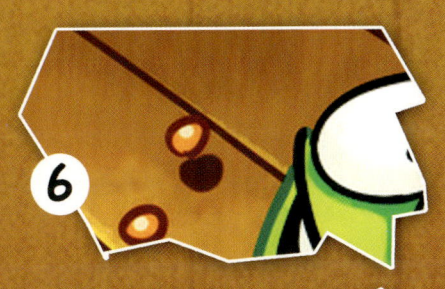

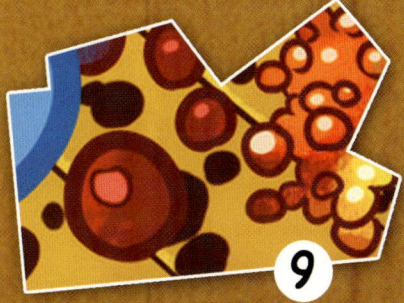

37

Om Nom's 'Feed Me' Flipbook

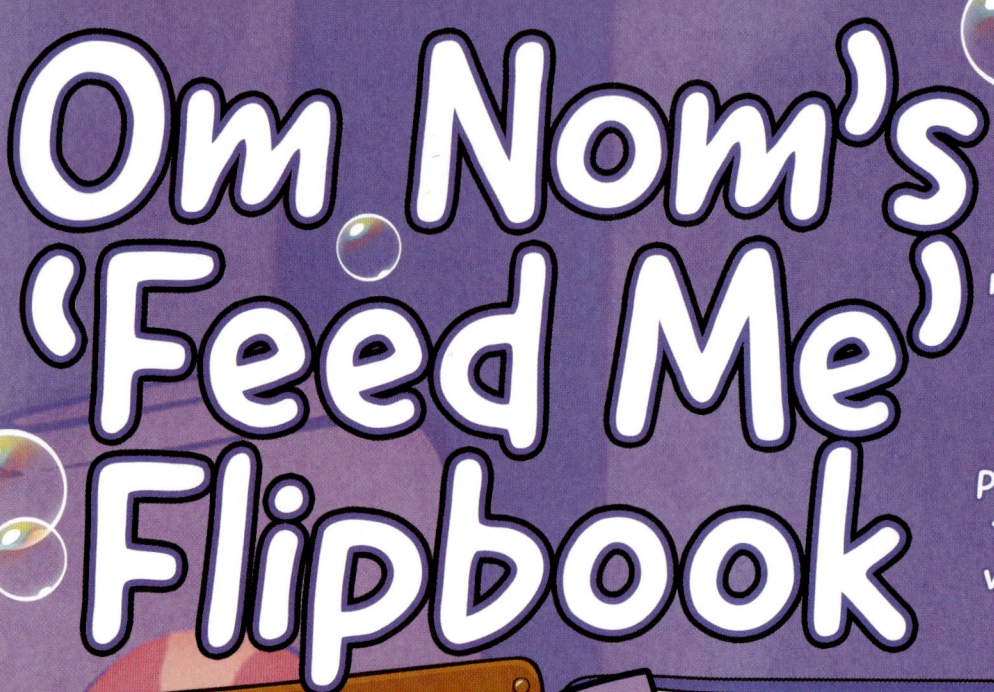

Make your own mini-movie starring Om Nom! Flipbooks work in the same way as cartoons. By drawing a picture on each page and then flipping the pages very fast, you can make your characters move.

You will need
Unwanted notebook or pad.
Pencil
Colouring pens

1 Starting on the last page of the notebook, copy picture 1 onto the bottom right-hand corner of the page.

2 Turn to the next page from the back of the notebook, and draw picture 2 in the same position.

3 Keep copying the sequence of pictures, each one on a fresh page, until you have drawn them all.

4 Now use your thumb to flip from the back of the notebook to the front. You should see Om Nom gobbling up his candy in front of your eyes!

1
2
3
4
5
6
7
8
9
10
11
12

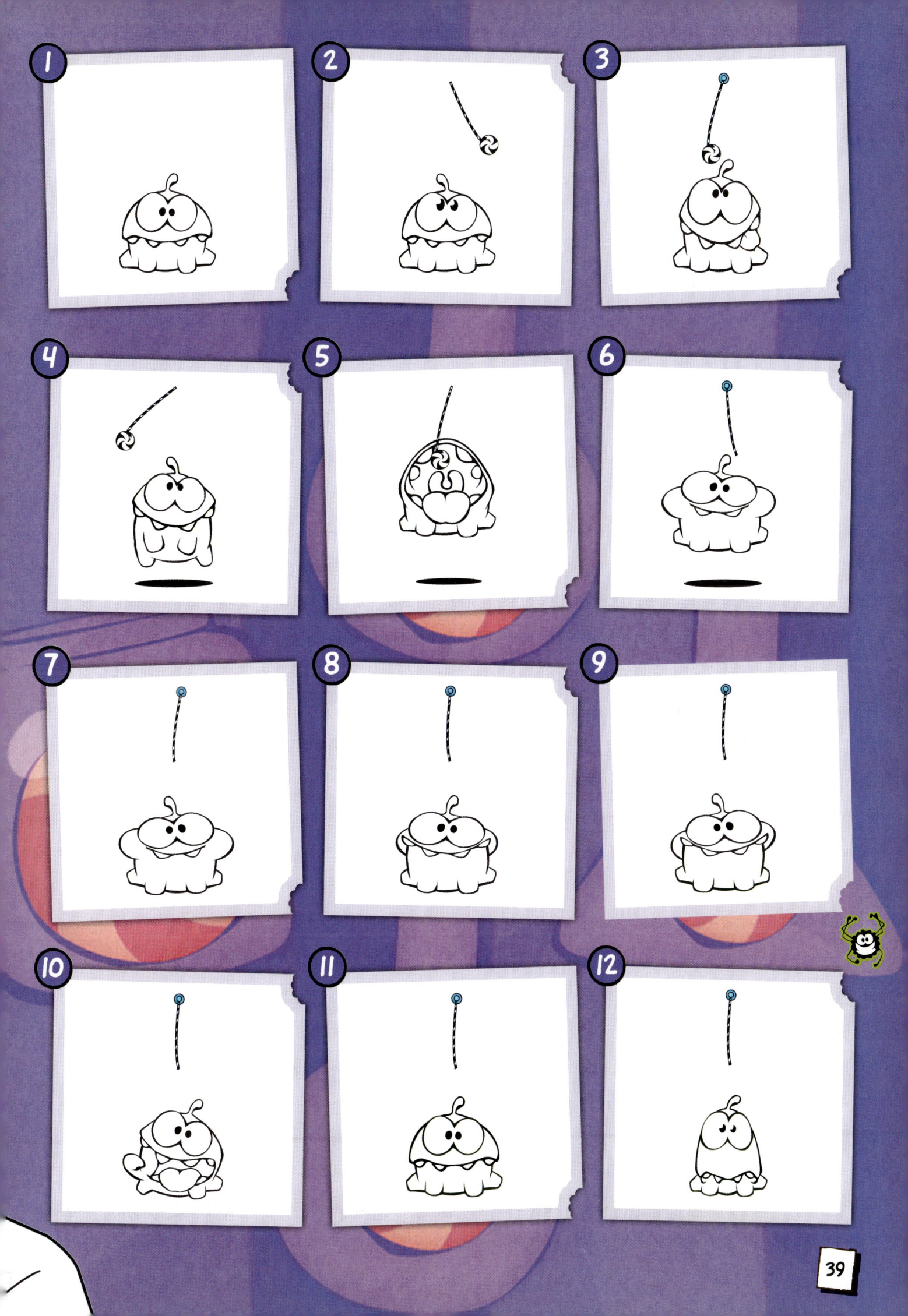

39

Colour By Numbers

Evan, Haley and the Professor are trying to protect Om Nom from kidnappers. But the bad guys have just turned up! Use the colour code to complete this exciting scene.

1. 2. 3. 4.
5. 6. 7. 8.
9. 10.

41

OM NOM

CUT the ROPE

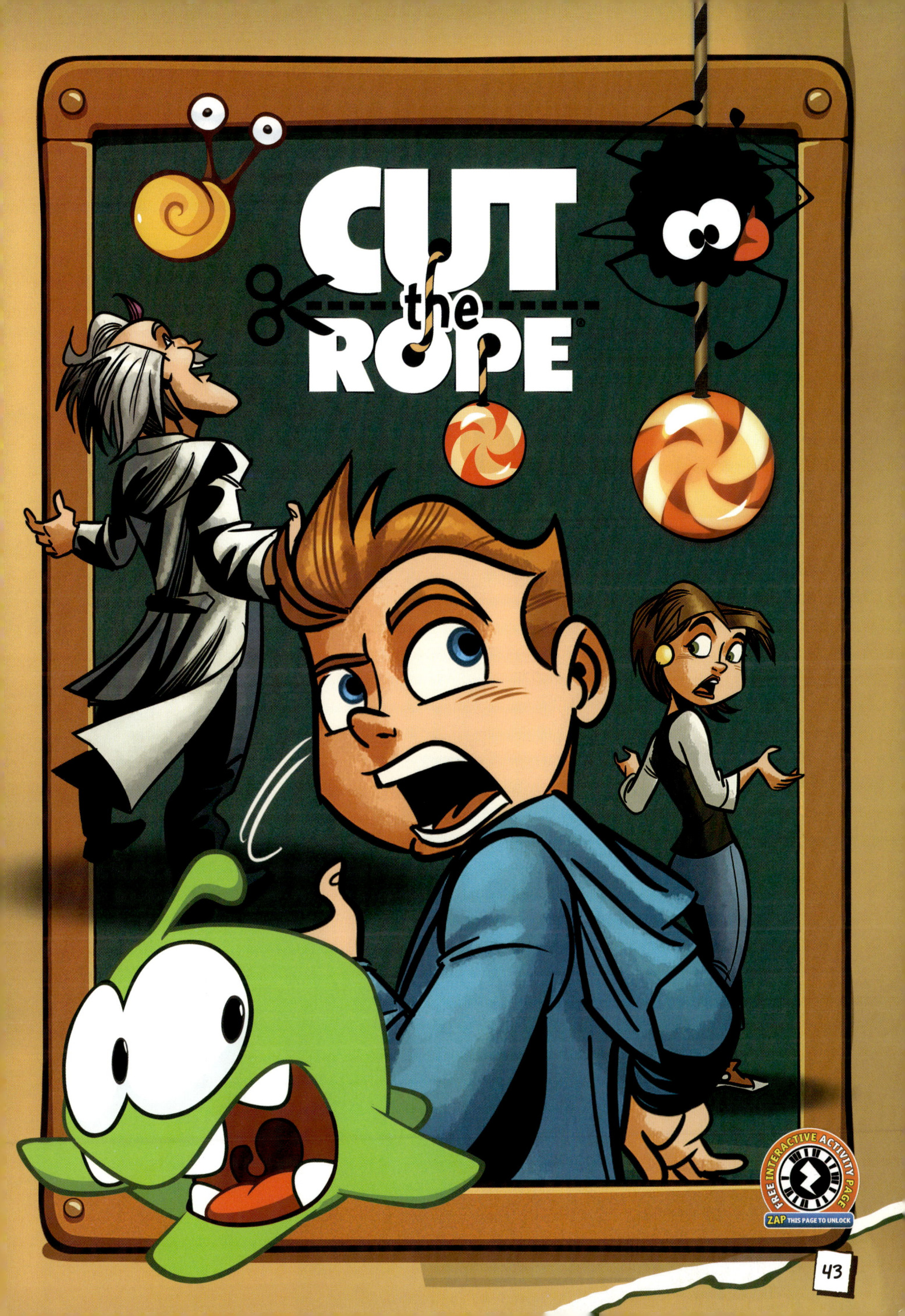

Time Travel

Om Nom is travelling through time to find the very best candy ever made. But will he reach these amazing sweets before Spider catches up with him? It's up to you to help him get there first.

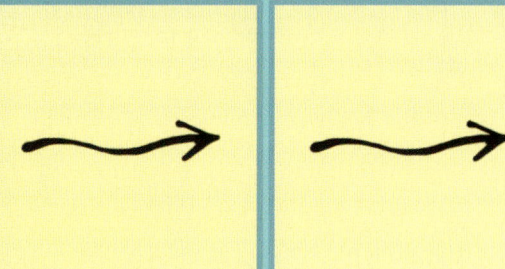

START

Oops! You have travelled back forty years instead of eighty years. Next time you throw the dice, halve the number your throw.

You find a clue in an ancient pyramid. Next time you throw the dice, double the number your throw.

You stop to battle a dragon and meet a princess. Go back two spaces.

A pirate tries to make you walk the plank. Go back five spaces.

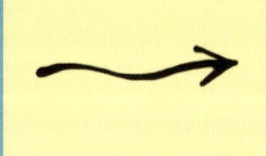

FINISH

You spot the candy! Go forward three spaces.

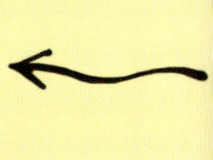

44

Equipment
• Dice • Markers • Two or more players

How to Play
1. Choose which player will take the first turn.
2. Throw the dice and enter the time vortex.
3. Follow any instructions you land on.
4. The winner is the first player to find the best candy ever made.

You land in a castle moat. *Miss a turn.*

You pose for a famous artist. *Swap marker places with the player on your right.*

You meet a Tyrannosaurus Rex. *Run forward four spaces. Quickly!*

You make friends with a Brontosaurus. *Have another turn.*

Spider has reached the candy first. *Go back to the start and try again.*

45

Time Tangle

Om Nom is lost in time! Follow the rope with your finger to find out where he is stuck.

1
2
3
4
5

HOW TO DRAW OM NOM

Follow these simple steps and learn how to draw your favourite little green monster!

1. Start with the eyes. Use a pencil first, and then go over the lines with a black felt tip.

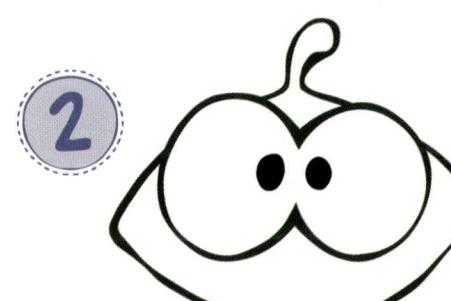

2. Add Om Nom's head in the same way. Notice the places where the black line looks thicker or thinner.

3. Now draw the teeth. Make sure that you space them evenly.

4. Carefully sketch three lines to create Om Nom's body. Keep going over your pencil line with black felt tip.

5. Add the feet and then colour Om Nom's body. Look carefully – you will need TWO shades of green!

47

Shadow Match

Om Nom knows who his friends are. He can even tell them apart in the dark! Can you identify these shadows?

1.
2.

48

49

Anagrams

1. Om Nom likes eating wesets.

2. Chocolate makes tornmess happy.

3. Om Nom is small, green and hisqyus.

4. Om Nom needs to eat every five meistun.

5. Sipmobiles things can come true!

6. My first experiment began with pucesack...

Om Nom has chewed up the Professor's paperwork in his hunt for candy. Can you help the Professor to save his research by unscrambling these muddled notes?

UNSCRAMBLED WORDS

1.
2.
3.
4.
5.
6.

Sweet Thief!

Spider has eaten Om Nom's lunch! Can you put the pieces in the right order and find out what Spider stole?

1. K
2. A
3. E
4. C

The correct order for the numbers is

Spider ate a

Strange Delivery

Part 2

"...You have to stay here while I go spend the day at the place I'm still not convinced isn't some CRAZILY ELABORATE and LONG punishment for all the nights I kept my parents awake after I was born.

They say it's "SCHOOL". I say that's what they want me to believe."

BRIIINNNGGGG

"HEY EVAN! WAIT UP!"

"YEAH. WHY DO YOU ASK?"

"WELL FOR ONE, YOU FELL ASLEEP IN CLASS. AND NOT JUST IN ANY CLASS. YOU FELL ASLEEP IN MS. DOYLE'S CLASS."

"SO, IS IT OKAY IF I COME BY AFTER SCHOOL?"

"OH...YEAH. TOTALLY."

"ARE YOU OKAY?"

YESSSS! HALEY'S COMING OVER! AGAIN!
YOU KNOW, IT JUST OCCURRED TO ME.
I HAVE NO IDEA WHAT YOUR NAME IS. OR IF YOU EVEN HAVE ONE.
OM NOM.
WE SHOULD NAME YOU. RIGHT NOW.
OM NOM.
LET'S SEE. HM...
I GOT IT! GLOBBY!
OM NOM.
CLARENCE!
OM NOM.
COUNT CHOCULA!
OM NOM.
WAIT! WHAT DID YOU JUST SAY?
OM NOM.
OM NOM? HMM...NOT BAD. NOT BAD AT ALL.
OM NOM.

PROJECT: NUTRILICIOUS HAS BEEN DELAYED LONG ENOUGH. HAVE WE RECEIVED ANY WORD FROM THE CATCHER BROTHERS?
NOTHING YET, SIR.
WE DO KNOW THEY'VE ARRIVED AT THE LOCATION THE SUBJECT IS BELIEVED TO BE.
IT'S THE ADDRESS THAT WEIRDO HIPPYISH DELIVERY DRIVER GAVE US, BROTHER ZEB.
THAT'S THE PROFESSOR AND IT LOOKS LIKE HE'S LEAVIN'!
AFTER WE GRAB THIS LITTLE GREEN THING, WE SHOULD GET US SOME STRAWBERRY MILKSHAKES.
BROTHER ZEB, YOU ARE SPEAKING MY LANGUAGE!

WE'VE GOT A PROBLEM!
WHAT'S GOING ON?
THERE'S THESE TWO CREEPY GUYS SNEAKING AROUND YOUR NEIGHBOR'S HOUSE.
THAT'S PROFESSOR VANKIN'S HOUSE. I'VE GOT THIS THEORY THAT IT'S SORT OF A MAGNET FOR CREEPY WEIRDNE--
THEY WERE TALKING ABOUT CAPTURING A LITTLE GREEN THING.
THEY WANT TO CAPTURE OM NOM?
WHAT PART OF THE WORD "SUBTLE" DON'T YOU UNDERSTAND, BROTHER ZEB?!?
UHH.. ALL OF IT.
JUST GET IN THE HOUSE.
YESSIR, BROTHER ZED!
WOULDN'T IT JUST BE SMARTER TO STAY IN MY HOUSE?
I MEAN, IF THEY THINK OM NOM IS IN HERE, THEN THEY DON'T KNOW HE'S ACTUALLY AT MY HOUSE.
A MORE CONSISTENT EATING SCHEDULE WILL PREVENT SUCH OVERINDULGENCE IN THE FUTURE.
THERE'S A TALKING REFRIGERATOR. THAT'S NORMAL FOR THIS PLACE, RIGHT?

OOOF!
AHH!
OWW!
NOT SO FAST!
HEY BROTHER ZEB, WHAT DO YOU THINK WE SHOULD DO WITH THESE TWO?
HOP!
WHA...?
THUMP!
OW!
OM NOM!
OWWWWW!
WHAP!
LET'S GO!
WHAT DO WE DO NOW?!?
NO IDEA! LET'S JUST GET OUT OF HERE!
OM NOM!
WE'LL BE TAKING "OM NOM" FROM HERE!

THE CATCHER BROT
FOLLOW THAT CAR!
YOU'VE ALWAYS WANTED TO SAY THAT, HAVEN'T YOU?
THE CATCHER BROTHERS
AH-AH-AH-AH!
junka
junka
junka
AH-AH-AH-AH-AH!
unkajunkajunkajunk
KE-RAWRSH!
ARE YOU PEOPLE MAD!? YOU NEARLY DESTROYED MY LATEST ACQUISITION!
HEY!

KEEP PEDALLING, THERE'S NO WAY THEY CAN CATCH UP NOW!
SNAP!
REALLY!?
TOO MUCH WEIGHT! RUN FOR IT!
WHOA WHOA WHOA, I DON'T "RUN".
SIGH
NOT MUCH FARTHER.
WE CAN LOSE THEM IN THE CORN MAZE.
TELL ME YOU KNOW YOUR WAY OUTTA HERE.
NOT REALLY. THEY CHANGE IT UP EVERY YEAR.
AWESOME.
DESPITE POPULAR BELIEF, CORN IS NOT IN FACT A VEGETABLE, BUT A GRAIN.
THIS THING MUST BE MOTION ACTIVATED.
IT'S GONNA GIVE US AWAY IF WE'RE NOT CAREFUL.

THE WAY I FIGURE IT, BROTHER ZEB, WE NEED ONLY TO FOLLOW THE TOTEM VOICE AND THAT WILL LEAD US STRAIGHT TO OUR PRIZE!
BRILLIANT, BROTHER ZED!
THERE'S GOTTA BE AN OFF BUTTON SOMEWHERE.
YOU KNOW, HALEY, I'M PRETTY SURE ANY OF THESE EXITS WILL GET US OUTTA HERE.
DO NOT REMOVE
BUT IF WE CHOOSE THE OBVIOUS PATH, THEY'LL BE RIGHT ON OUR HEELS.
CORN, WHEN USED AS A TOPICAL, CAN PREVENT ARTHRITIS AS WELL AS BOREDOM.
IS THAT EVEN TRUE, BROTHER ZED?
SHOOSH! WE'RE GETTING CLOSE!
CORN WILL ONE DAY REPLACE RAIN AS EARTH'S PRIMARY PRECIPITATION.
AROOOOOOOOOOOO
UH-OH.
CGPD
WHAT SEEMS TO BE THE PROBLEM, ER, OFFICERS?
EXCESSIVE SPEEDING IN A RESIDENTIAL, HIT AND RUN, RECKLESS ENDANGERMENT, I DON'T KNOW WHERE TO BEGIN.
WE CAN EXPLAIN, RIGHT, BROTHER ZED?
OF COURSE!
FREE INTERACTIVE STORY PAGE
ZAP THIS PAGE TO UNLOCK

EVERYBODY LOVES OM NOM!

Would you like a cute little monster hiding out in your room, just like Evan? Now you can make an Om Nom who will sit on your desk and watch over your sweets!

You will need
- A thick piece of white card
- Colouring pens/paints
- Pencil
- Scissors
- Saucer
- Sticky tape

1 Carefully pencil the template onto the piece of card. Don't forget to draw the tab at the bottom.

2 Use paints or felt tips to colour in your monster.

3 Ask an adult to help you cut out the figure, including the tab.

4 Fold the tab back under the figure to make it stand up.

5 Stick the tab to the edge of a saucer.

6 Fill the saucer with sweets and ask Om Nom to guard them for you!

Always ask an adult to help you when using scissors and safety pins.

Fold tab under

Fold tab under

DOUGHNUT

DROP

Om Nom's enemies are trying to catch him by dropping doughnuts all over the town. Evan has to find them all before Om Nom does! Help him search for the doughnuts and write down how many you find.

I can see _____ doughnuts.

COOKIE CUTTER

Baking is fun! If you're anything like Evan and Om Nom, you'll love these yummy cookies. Ask an adult to help you make them.

You will need
- 150g sugar
- 140g butter
- 1 tsp vanilla extract
- Pinch of nutmeg
- 1 large egg, beaten
- 220g plain flour
- 3/4 tsp baking powder
- 200g chocolate chips
- Handful mixed chopped nuts (optional)

1 Preheat the oven to 180 C.

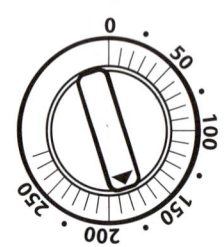

2 Line a baking sheet with greaseproof paper.

3 Cream together the butter and sugar until fluffy.

4 Add the egg, nutmeg and vanilla extract and mix well.

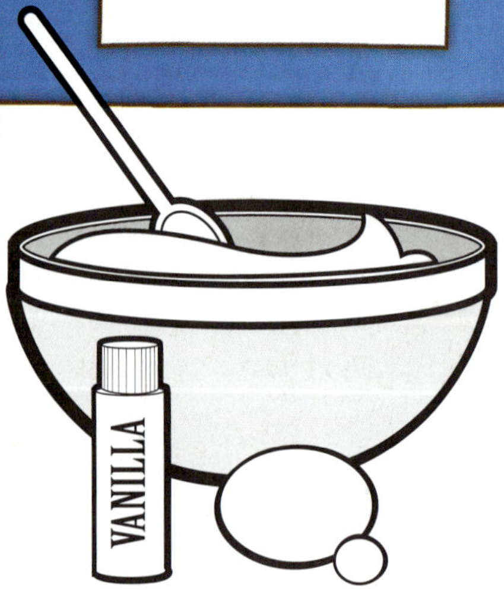

5 Sieve the flour and baking powder into the bowl and mix again.

Always ask an adult to help you when using the oven.

6. Add the chocolate chips and nuts (if using) to the mixture and stir them in.

7. Place heaped teaspoons of the cookie dough on the baking sheets.

8. Bake for 10 minutes or until light golden brown.

9. Cool on a wire tray.

10. Enjoy with a glass of cold milk!

Feed Me NOW!

Something has gone wrong with one of the Professor's experiments! The candy is there, but the ropes have gone missing. Can you draw the ropes in the right places so that Om Nom can have his dinner?

What's in the Box?

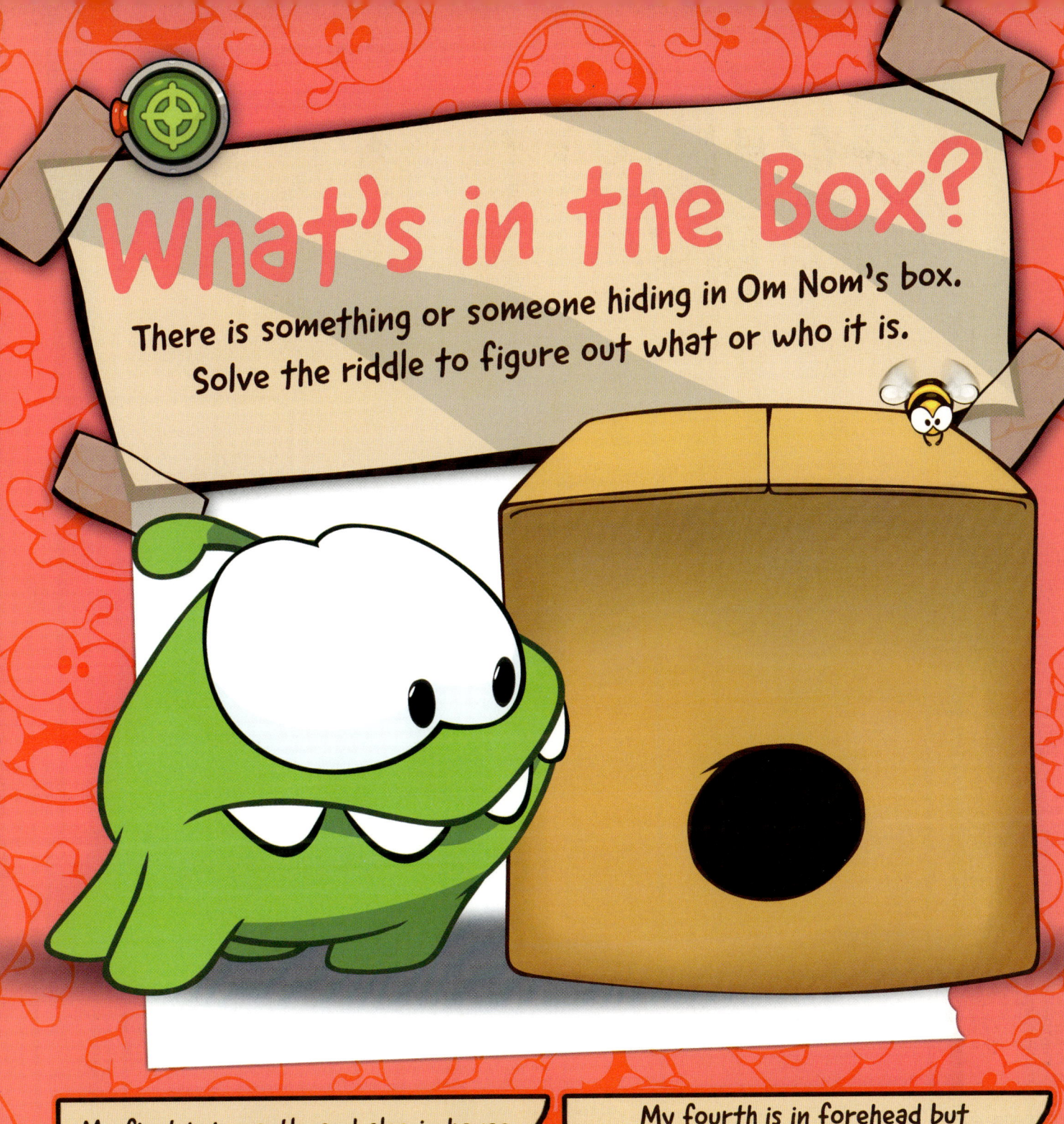

There is something or someone hiding in Om Nom's box. Solve the riddle to figure out what or who it is.

My first is in castle and also in house.

My second is in chipmunk but never in mouse.

My third is in snowing and mittens and skis.

My fourth is in forehead but never in knees.

My fifth is in breaks and also in bends.

My sixth is in riddles and that's where this ends!

IS INSIDE THE BOX!

Comical Candy

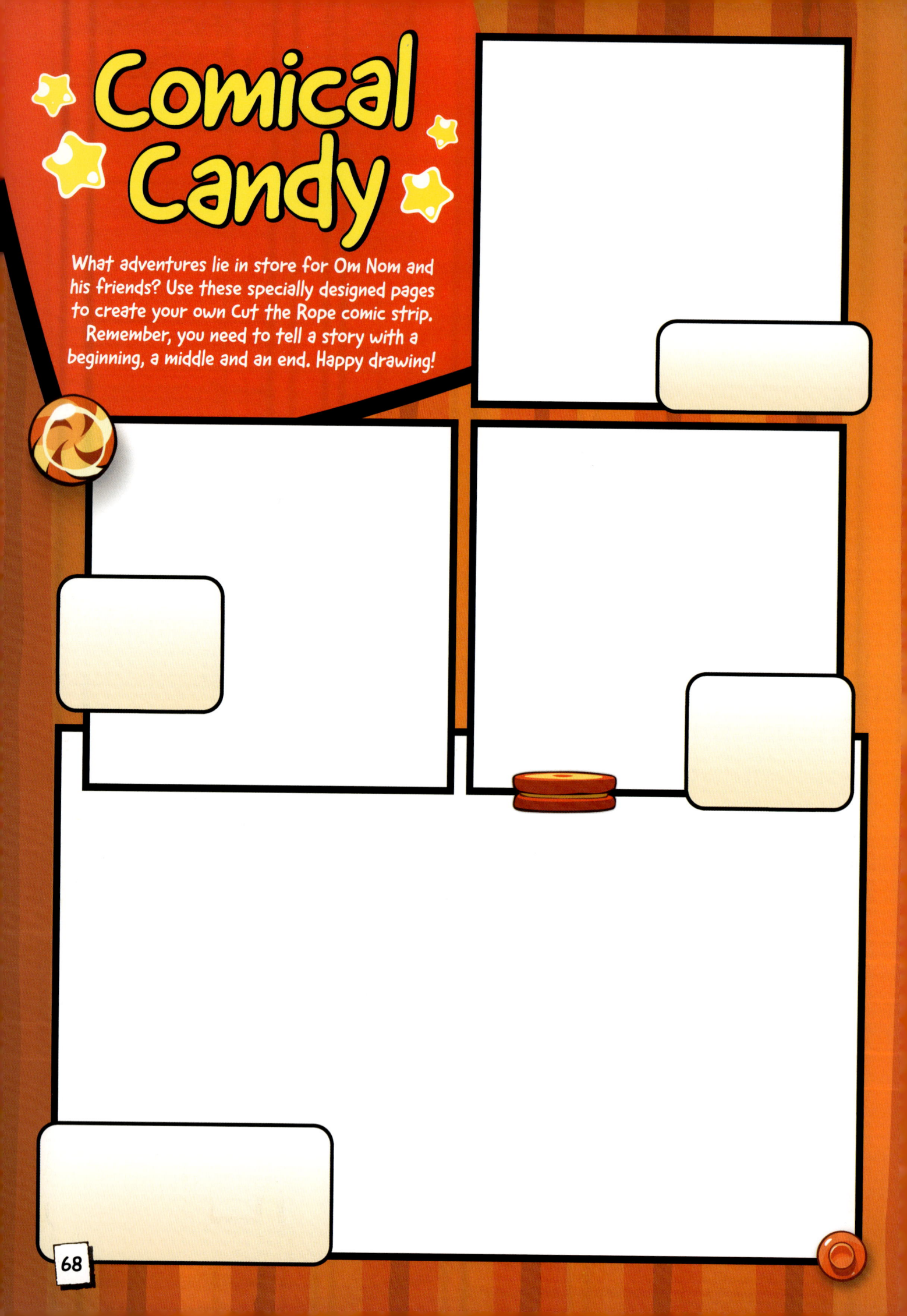

What adventures lie in store for Om Nom and his friends? Use these specially designed pages to create your own Cut the Rope comic strip. Remember, you need to tell a story with a beginning, a middle and an end. Happy drawing!

69

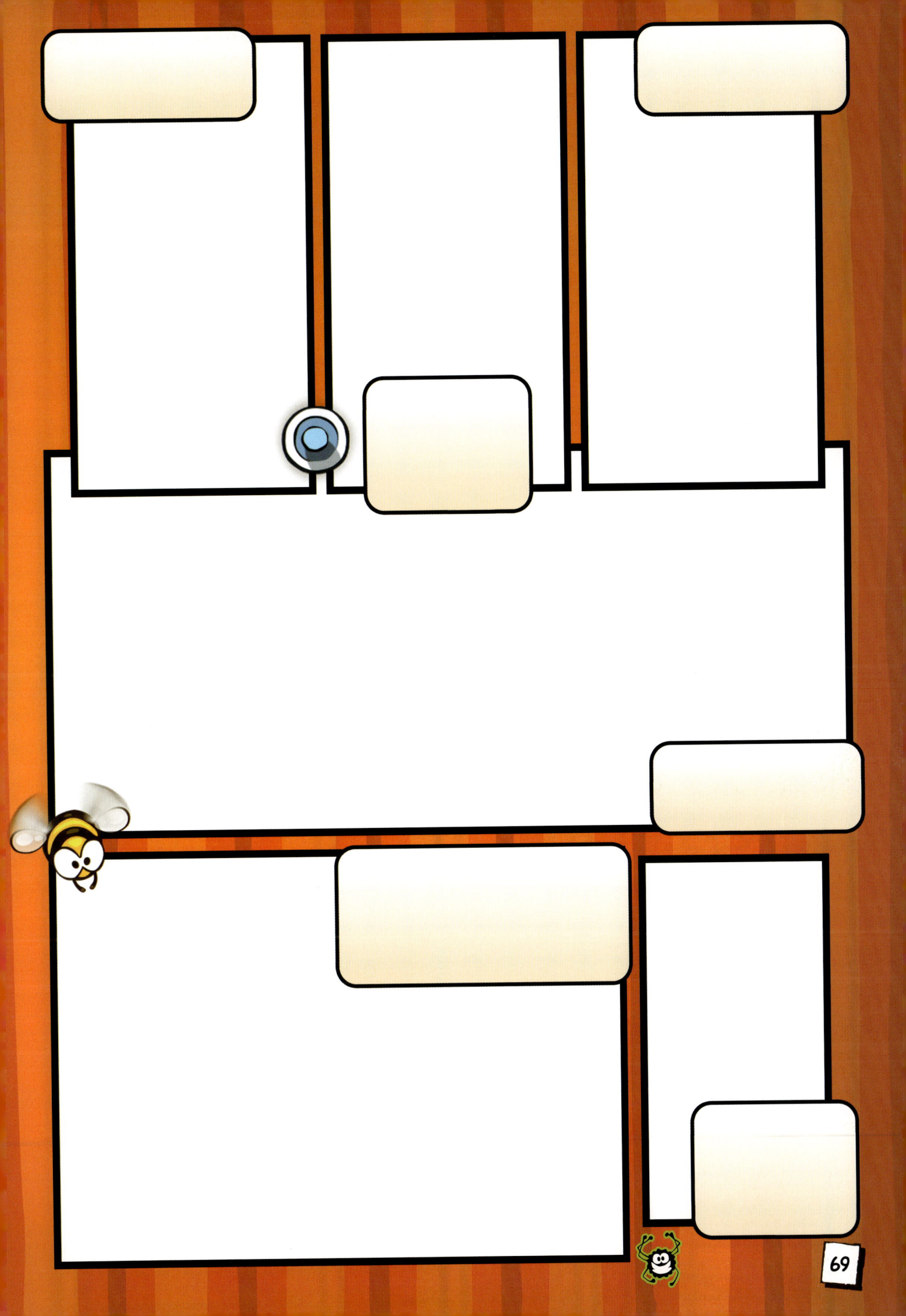

SWEET SUDOKU

This Sudoku square will tempt your taste buds! There are nine tasty treats looking for a home. Each row and column must include all nine pictures. Each small 3 x 3 square must also include the nine pictures.

Odd One Out

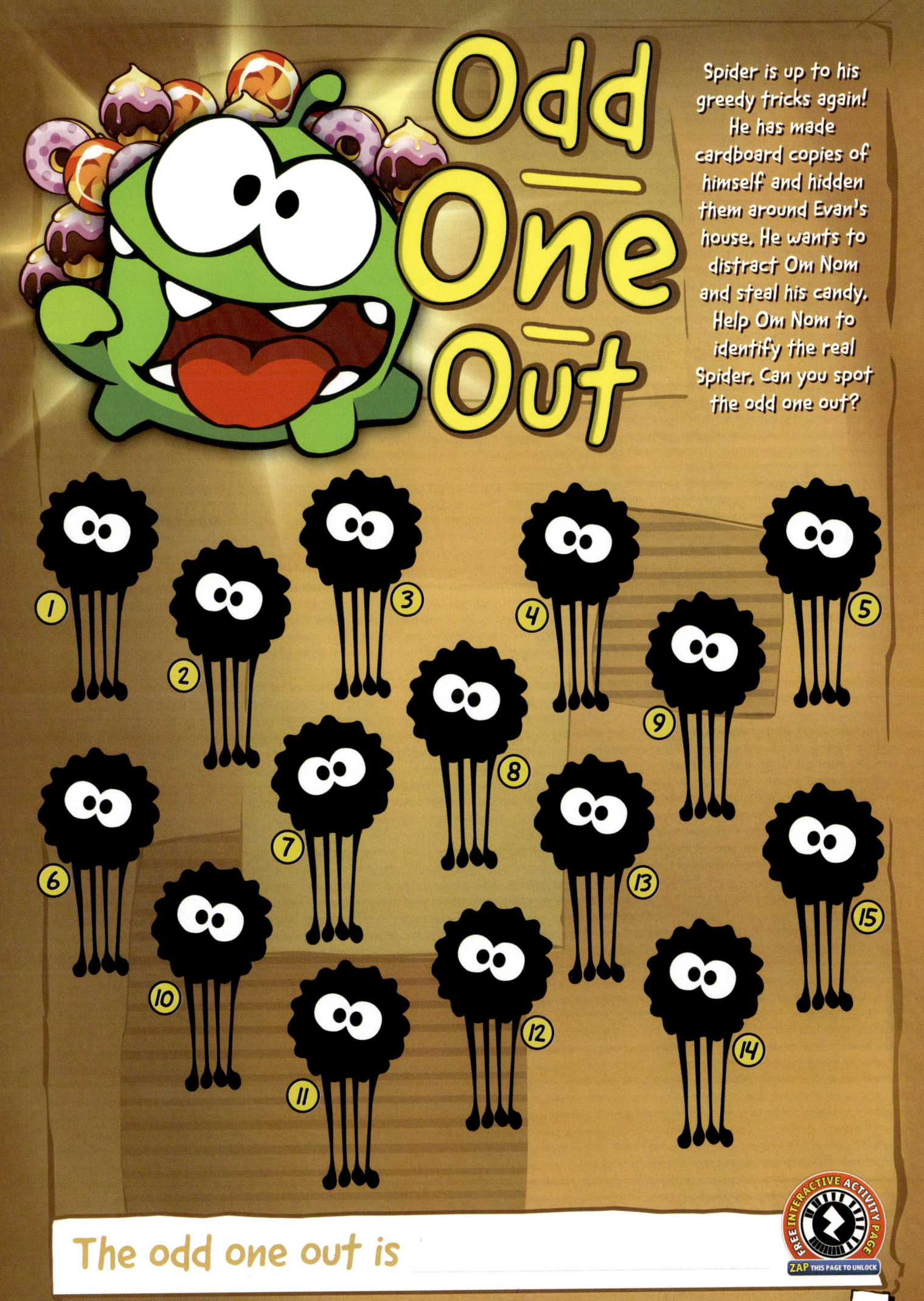

Spider is up to his greedy tricks again! He has made cardboard copies of himself and hidden them around Evan's house. He wants to distract Om Nom and steal his candy. Help Om Nom to identify the real Spider. Can you spot the odd one out?

The odd one out is

CREATIVE CATCHPHRASE

Evan loves making up funny phrases and weird exclamations. How many words can you make from this favourite saying of his?

OCTOPUS DINGLEBERRY!

Extreme Close-up!

Look carefully at these photos. Can you tell who has been snapped? Test your observation skills and try to name the character in each picture.

A

B

C

D

E

F

Brilliant Boxes

Evan knows that boxes can be exciting things – especially when they contain hungry monsters! Follow these steps to make your very own box.

You will need
Thick card
Pencil
Scissors
Glue
Paints
Paintbrushes
Black pen

Instructions

1. Copy the box template onto the card. The unbroken lines show where to cut. The dotted lines show where to fold.

2. Cut out your box and ask an adult to help you score along the fold lines. This will make them easier to fold.

3. Use your paints to decorate the template. You can copy one of Om Nom's boxes or create your own special design.

4. Decide what the label will say, and then write it using a black pen.

5. Wait for the paint to dry. Then glue the tabs and fold the template into a box shape.

What will your box be used for?

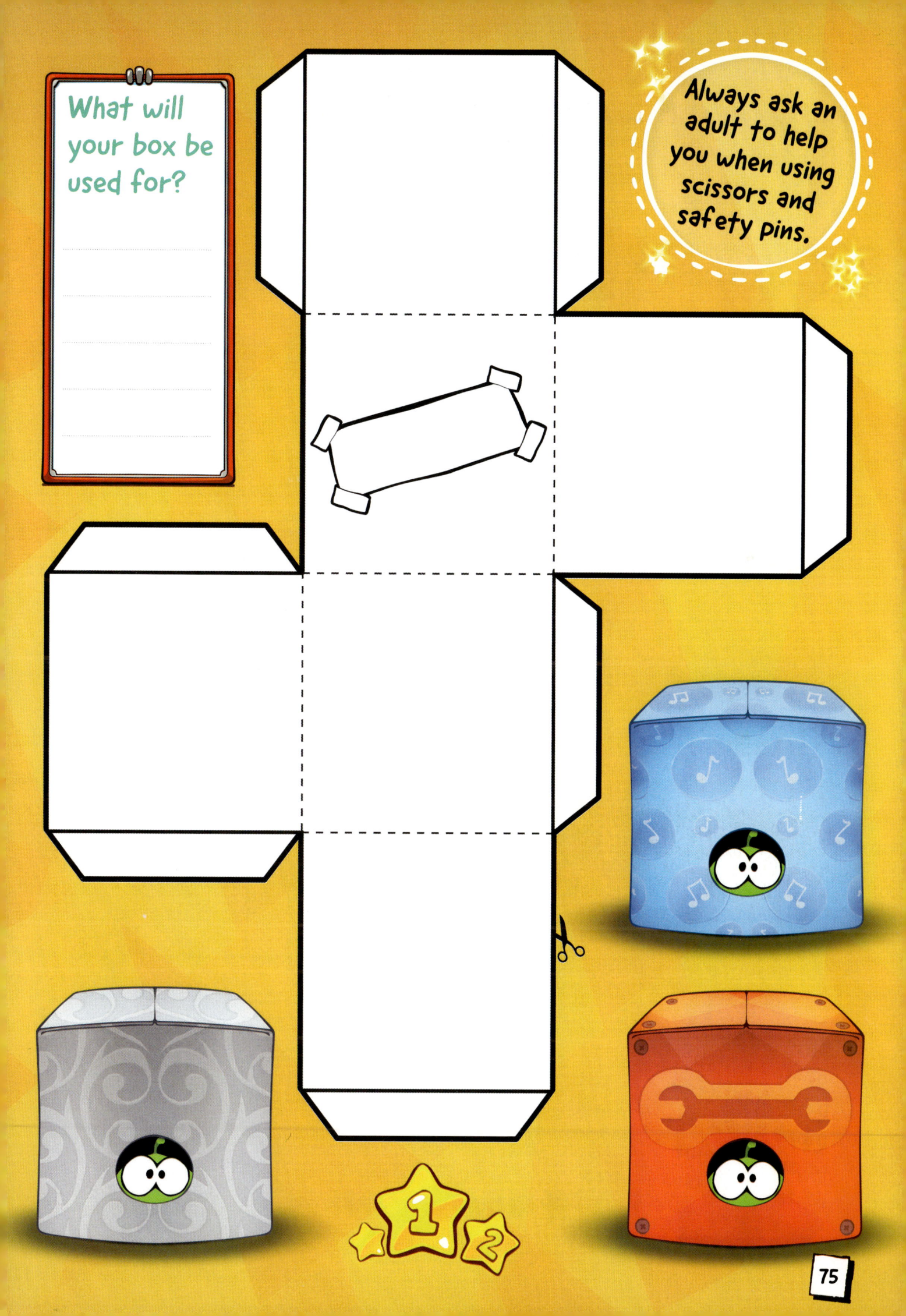

Always ask an adult to help you when using scissors and safety pins.

JELLY JIGSAW

The Professor has made an enormous jelly, and he wants to see how long it takes you to gobble the whole thing up!

Time how long it takes you to put the picture back together in the right way. As you work out where each piece belongs, write the number in the grid.

Answers

Pages 22–23

Page 32

Page 33
a3
b1
c4
d2

Page 51
CAKE

Pages 62–63
There are 17 doughnuts altogether.

Pages 67
Spider is in the box.

Page 70

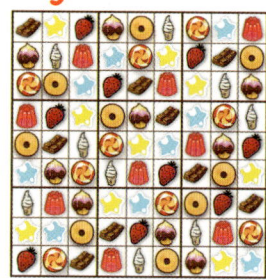

Page 71
7

Pages 34–35
1. The Professor 2. Sugar 3. Dentist 4. Almonds 5. Evan's dad
6. Lollipop 7. The aquarium 8. Spider 9. A box 10. Easter

Pages 36

Pages 37

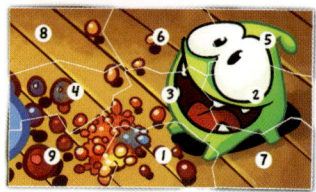

Page 73
a. Haley b. Om Nom c. Evan d. The Professor e. Snail f. Spider

Page 76

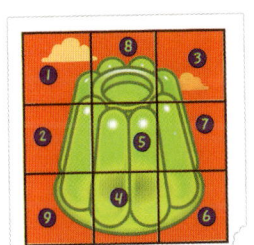

Page 46
Pirate Ship

Pages 48–49
1. Evan's dad 2. Evan 3. Professor 4. Haley 5. Spider 6. Evan's mum

Page 50
1. Om Nom likes eating sweets.
2. Chocolate makes monsters happy.
3. Om Nom is small, green and squishy.
4. Om Nom needs to eat every five minutes.
5. Impossible things can come true!
6. My first experiment began with cupcakes...

Pedigreebooks.com | ANNUALS | ACTIVITY

Cut the Rope Annual 2014

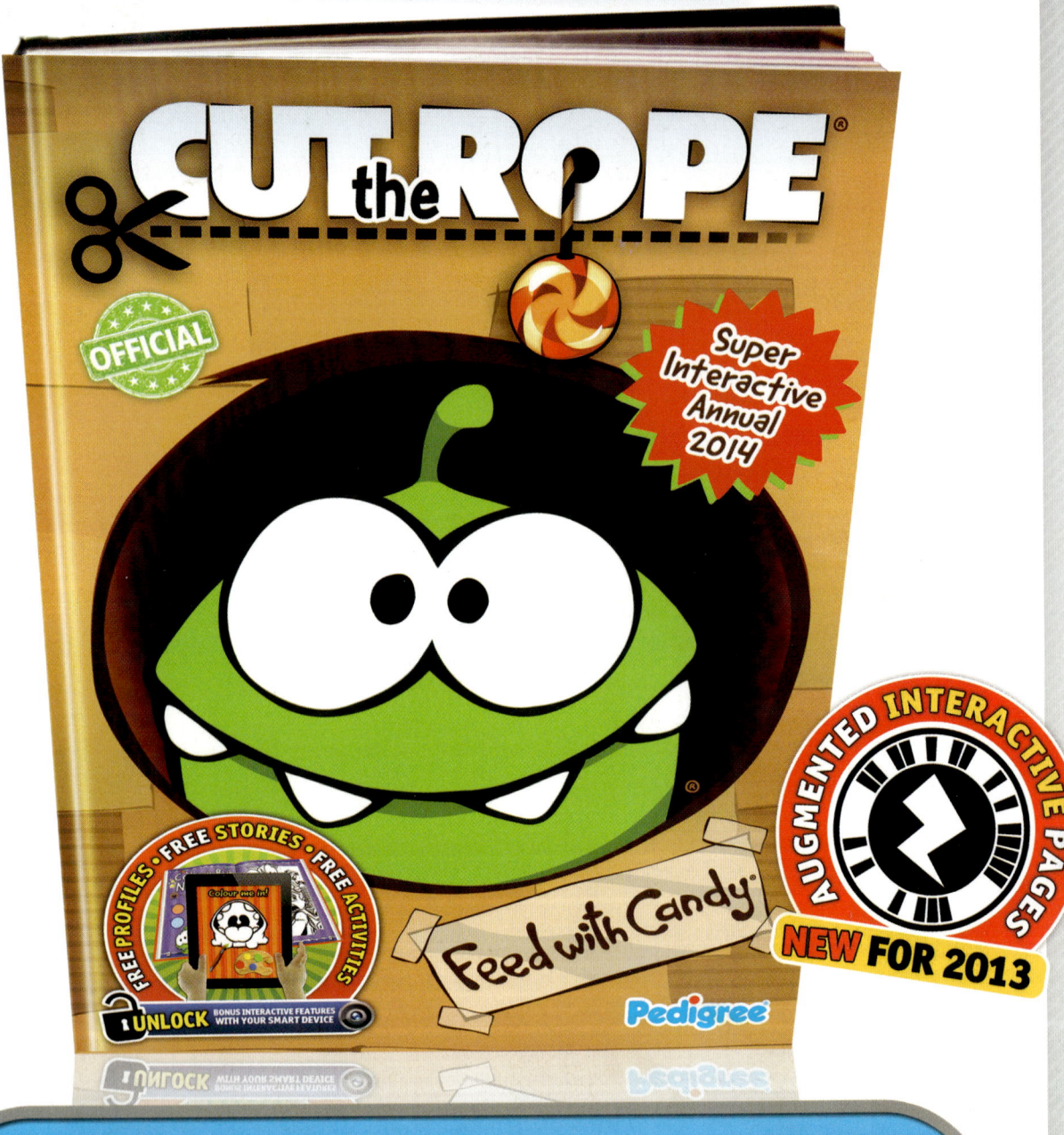

Visit **Pedigreebooks.com** to find out more on this year's **Cut the Rope Annual**, scan with your mobile device to learn more.

Visit www.pedigreebooks.com